Louise Bease

Allygaloo!

Making Music Together

by Alison Hedger

Songs, dances, poems and more....
Opportunities for exploring aspects of school music

Items suitable for all ages within the Primary sector

The pieces are excellent material for class and topic work, and concert items
(*Cross-curricular topic-link suggestions are given below in brackets)

CONTENTS

The accompanying CD allows schools to learn the songs quickly and practice the dances.
It is also suitable for performances.

A licence should be obtained from Music Sales Limited for performances of this work.

© Copyright 2000 Golden Apple Productions

A division of Chester Music Limited
8/9 Frith Street, London W1D 3JB

Order No. GA11176

ISBN 0-7119-8660-6

9.95

Alison Hedger has been successfully teaching and writing music for children, for many years. She has developed a particular style of teaching class music, which is both lively and full of fun. Alison believes that children quickly "catch" rhythm passed on by physical involvement with music. On the other hand, most children take time to imitate pitch correctly. Pulse, patterns (both rhythmic and melodic), structure, dynamics, imitation and creative thinking feature in Alison's lessons, and many games and songs require physical involvement.

ALLYGALOO! is a collection of some of Alison's favourite teaching material.
"I am fortunate in having a large open area in which to teach, so giving the children plenty of space in which to move. I am able to direct things from the piano, but I realise that this is not something available to many schools. However, the CD recording which is part of this book makes the dances and songs readily accessible to everyone. The CD also means that teachers can join in the activity, rather than be stuck at the piano.

I hope this lively collection will help give young children musical confidence and a secure skill base. But most of all, I hope in some small way, that the varied activities will help children develop a love for all things musical, so gaining a lifetime of enjoyment from the expressive arts. Have fun, and let the CD take the strain!"

Alison Hedger

ONE MAKING MUSIC TOGETHER

Making music together is our joy,
It brings pleasure to every girl and boy.
When we play and we sing, hear the music ring,
We are bathed in wonderful sound.

Making music together is great fun,
It binds ages and cultures into one.
When we play and we sing, all our cares take wing.
Happiness in music we have found.

INSTRUMENTAL SECTION

Repeat the instrumental melody, playing simultaneously with a repeat of the song

The instrumental section can be played on kazoos, or on any suitable pitched instruments, as available. It can also be sung to "la, la..."

The addition of a drum kit throughout, is ideal.

A musical introduction has been added on the CD, to help children to make a tidy entry to the song.

ONE MAKING MUSIC TOGETHER

Song with kazoo melody

Play first four bars as introduction

Brightly and with enthusiasm ♩ = 115

D Bm7 Em A D F♯m

Kazoos etc. *jauntily*

Mak-ing mu - sic to-geth - er is our joy, it brings plea - sure to eve - ry

mf

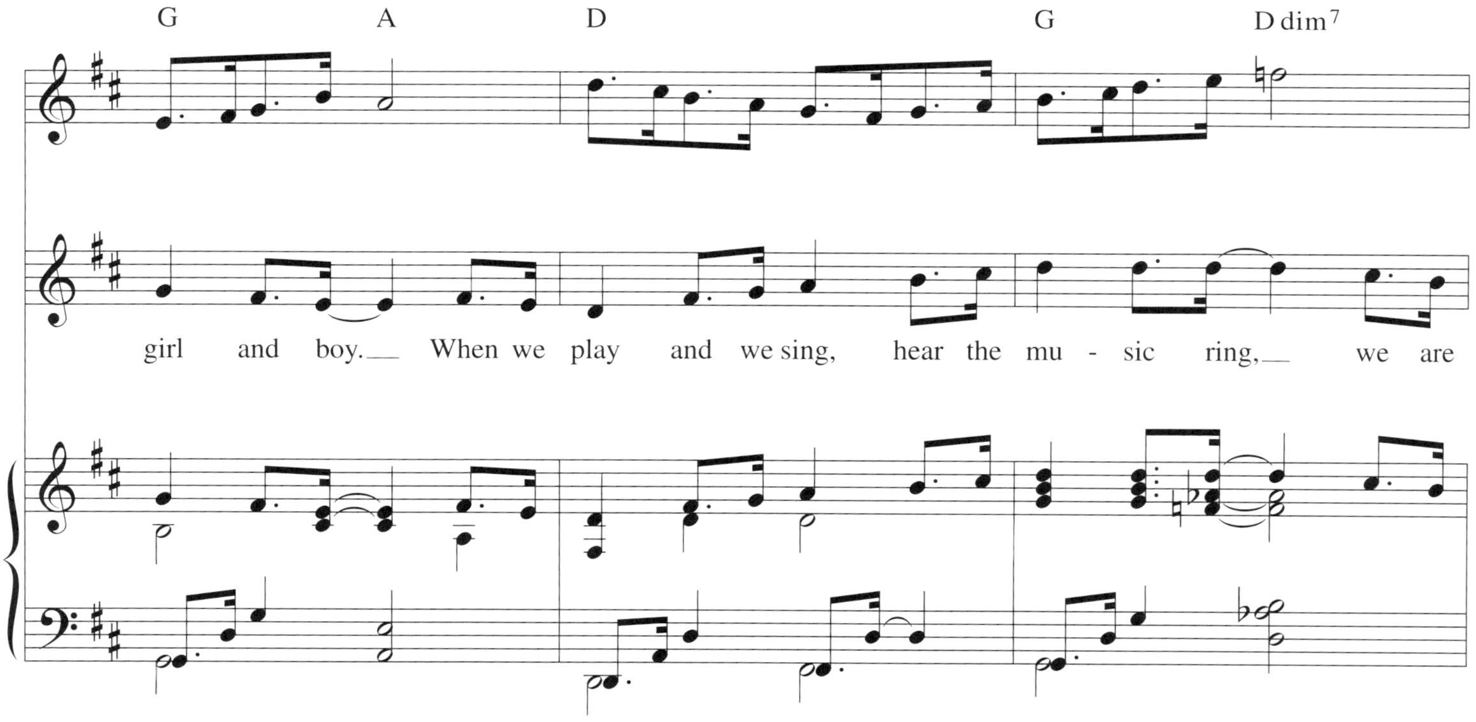

G A D G D dim7

girl and boy. When we play and we sing, hear the mu - sic ring, we are

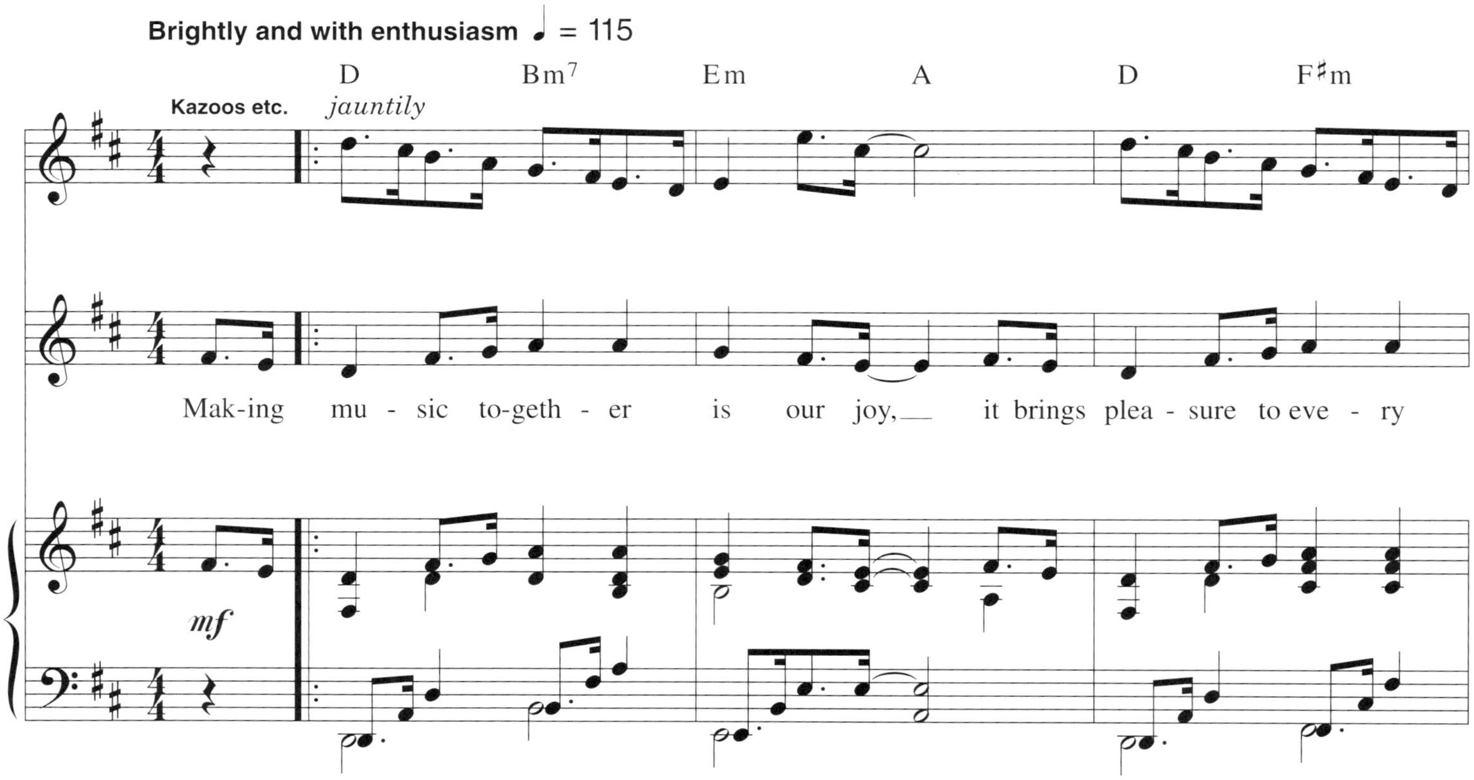

F♯m
F
A7
D
Bm7
bathed in won-der-ful sound. Mak-ing mu-sic to-geth-er

Em
A
D
F♯m
G
A
is great fun, it binds a-ges and cul-tures in-to one. When we

D
G
D dim7
F♯m
A
play and we sing, all our cares take wing. Hap - pi - ness in mu - sic we have

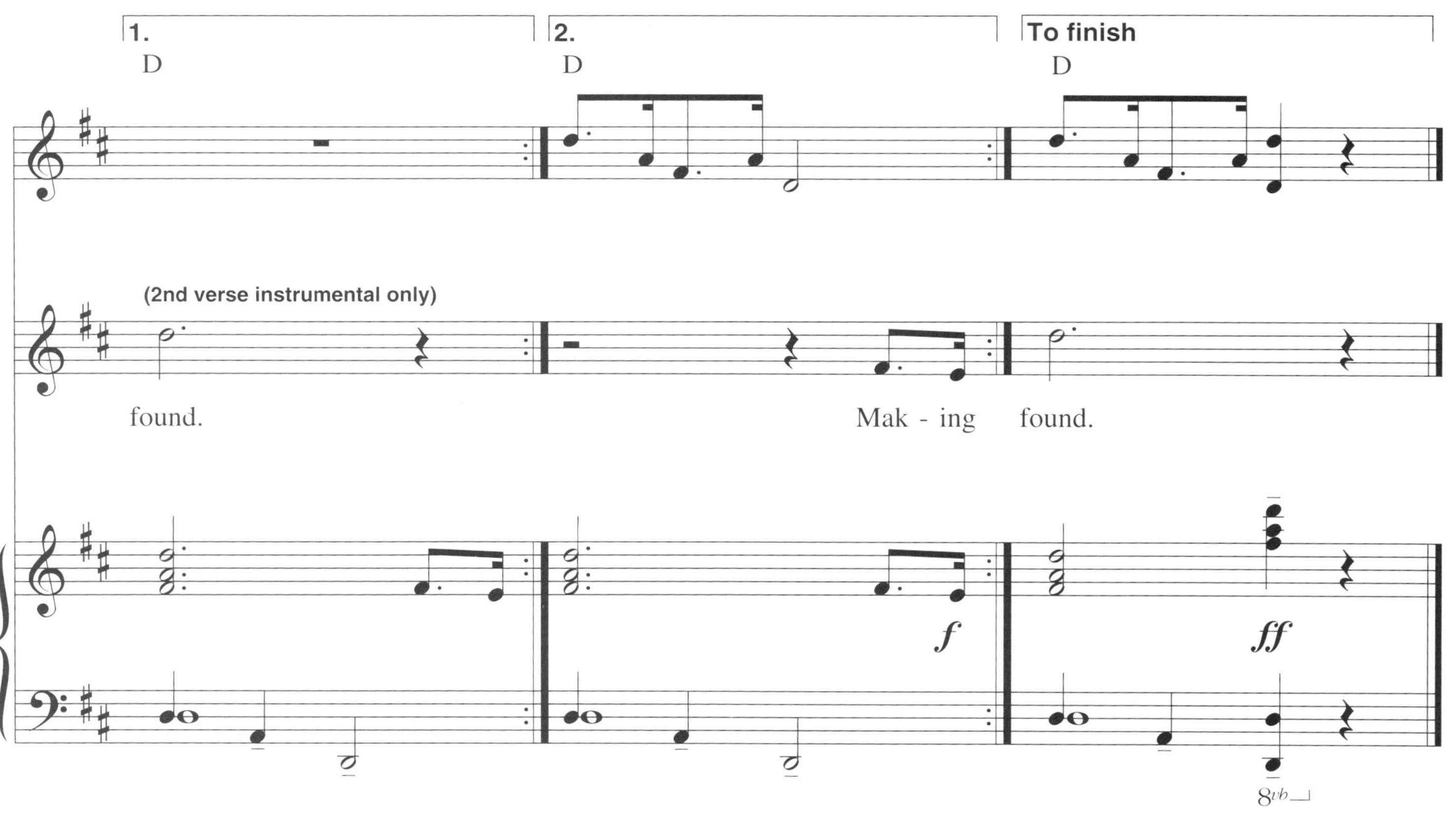
1.
2.
To finish
D
D
D
(2nd verse instrumental only)
found. Mak - ing found.
f
ff
8vb

TWO SAM, SUE AND SI

Poem to exercise vocal pitch

Use appropriate voices throughout

Sam, Sue and Si
Were eating a pie.

Said Sam very low, as he gave it a blow,
"This pie is quite hot,
But I like it a lot."

"Hey diddle diddle,
There's fruit in the middle"
Said Sue in her middling voice.

Cried Si, very high,
With his voice in the sky,
"This pastry is nice,
Can I have another slice?"

But there was no more pie,
So the three said goodbye,
In their voices,
Low, medium and high.

"Goodbye!" "Goodbye!" "Goodbye!"

THREE ALLYGALOO!

Actions:

The aim is to have children circling in contrary motion, so depicting a moving cog.

1. *Learn the song sitting on the floor.*
2. *Add actions to the last line, by turning lower arms around each other, in front of the chest, like a wheel. Clap once on the word "Oh!"*
3. *Stand up, on the spot, and sing and do actions as described above.*
4. *Make one large, standing circle. Sing the song (on the spot) using the actions known so far.*
5. *Keeping the circle, hold hands. Whilst singing take steps clockwise, until the last line, when the actions are done on the spot.*
6. *Repeat number 5, but this time the children turn on the spot as they rotate their arms.*
7. *Sing the song with all the actions known so far, but this time take up hands again after "Oh!", and rotate anti-clockwise as the song is repeated.*
8. *Sing the song through several times, with the actions making sure a good circle is maintained.*
9. *Now choose about one third of the children to make an inner circle, closing up the outer circle around them. The inner circle of children follow the pattern of the song exactly as before, but move in contrary motion to the outside circle. You now have your moving cog. Maintain the contrary motion: this is fun but needs concentration to keep regular circles.*
10. *Finally, if you have enough children, choose a few to be a third innermost circle. Their rotating will be as for the outside circle. The effect of a rotating cog will be memorable and enormous fun.*

THREE ALLYGALOO!

Circle dance song, imitating moving cogs

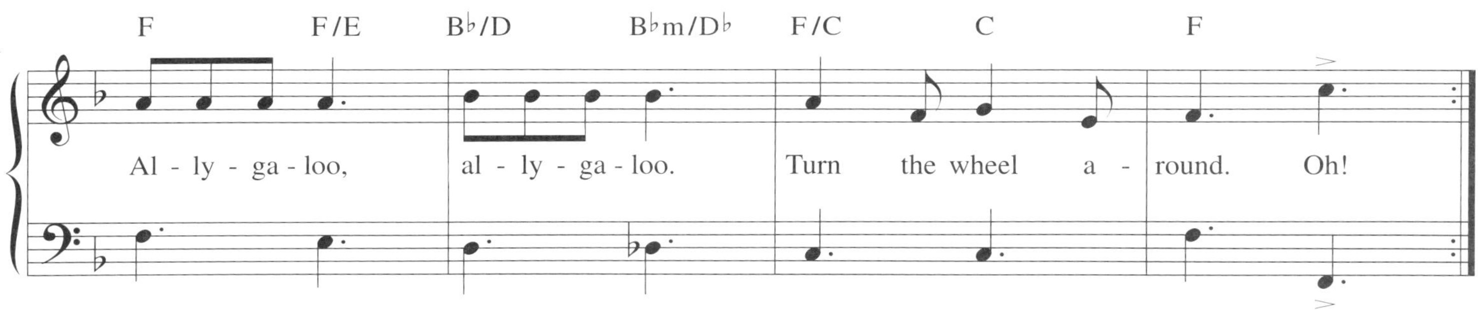

Allygaloo, galoo.
Allygaloo, galoo.
Allygaloo,
Allygaloo.
Turn the wheel around. Oh!

FOUR THE PENTATONIC DRAGON

Pitched percussion, rhyme and movement.

A group of children lie "asleep" on the floor, ready to become the dragon.
A group of musicians have pitched percussion instruments, using the five notes of the PENTATONIC SCALE.

The dragon lay still,
Was he dead or alive?
We crept softly forward and counted to five.

Softly play the five notes of the pentatonic scale, in ascending order, as children slowly and quietly count: **1 2 3 4 5**

When we got near,
We blew in his ear!

Quietly play the pentatonic scale in descending order, whilst the children whisper:
5 4 3 2 1
The children then blow gently like a summer breeze.

The dragon sat up
And gave us a smile.

A crash on a gong or suspended cymbal with a soft beater, as the dragon children sit up and give an enormous grin.

We kept very still
For quite a long while.

Silence and not a movement from anyone.

Then as it stood up (*it does*)
We started to run.
"Hey! Wait for me.
Let's have some good fun.
I love your music,
Let's play, dance and sing.
Jumble the notes –
Let the music begin."
So we played our five notes,
Any order was fine,
For a pentatonic dragon dance,
All in a line!

The dragon snakes in single file (hands on waist of one in front) dancing and singing, making up a song using a dragon voice as it goes. The musicians play any notes of the pentatonic scale at random, to be the accompaniment to the dragon's singing. Don't forget to add in the gong!

Repeat with different children being the dragon and musicians.

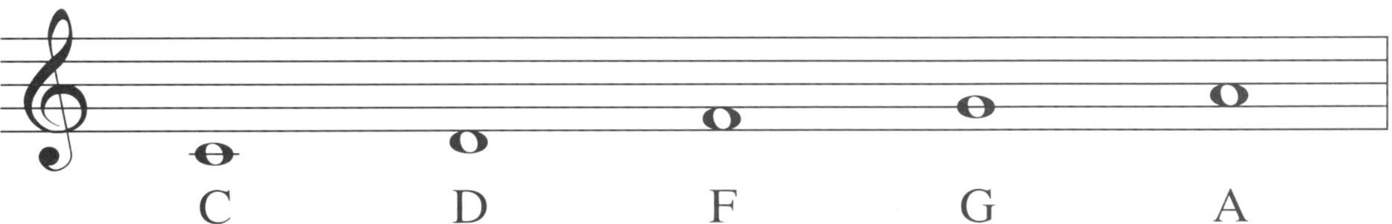

The ***PENTATONIC SCALE*** *has five notes. The Scottish Highland bagpipe is tuned to this scale and so these five notes are commonly used in Scottish melodies, e.g. Ye Banks And Braes O' Bonnie Doon. The pentatonic scale occurs in nearly all early musical cultures, and is thought to have been used in China as early as 2000 B.C.*

A special feature of creating music using the pentatonic scale, is that unlike tunes in major and minor scale, any or all of the notes played at the same time sound well together. This is particularly useful when children are composing.

Remember that a musical effect is dramatically altered by playing chime bars, xylophones, glockenspiels and metallophones with hard, medium or soft beaters.

FIVE LISTENING TO A MUSICAL SANDWICH!

Discerning bottom, middle and top tunes

The three tunes are presented on the accompanying CD. The idea is for the children to listen to the recording, and appreciate that one tune is low, one is high, and there is also a third tune in the middle. (Hence the referral to the whole as a sandwich.)

Tune One

The bottom melody played by a bassoon.

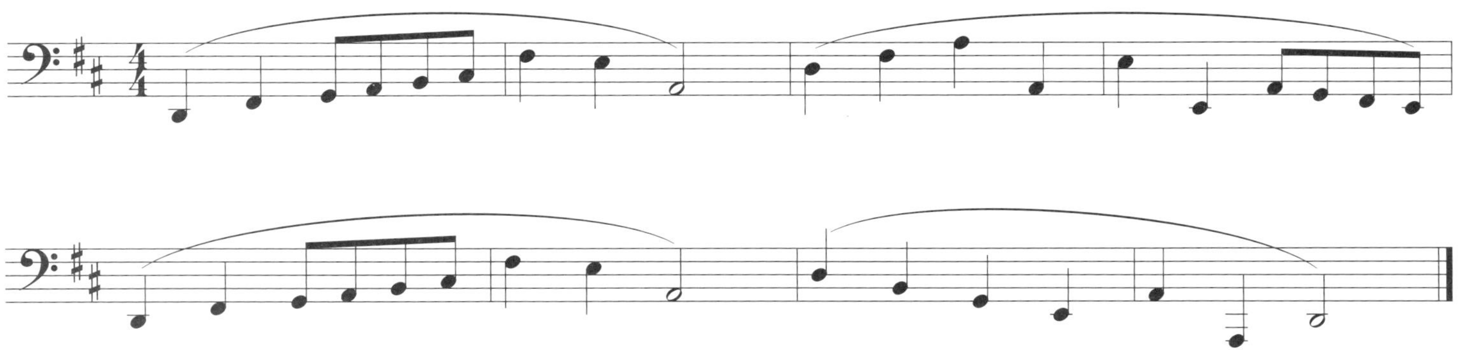

Tune Two

The middle melody played by an oboe.

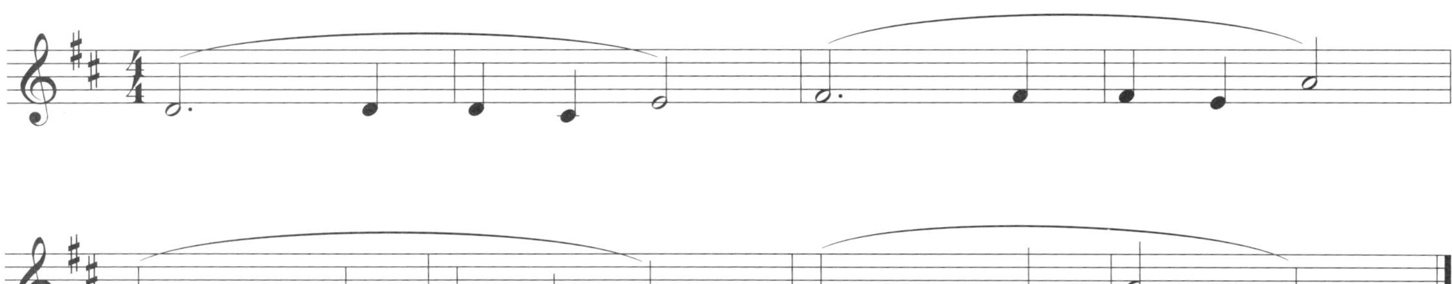

Tune Three

The top melody played by a flute.

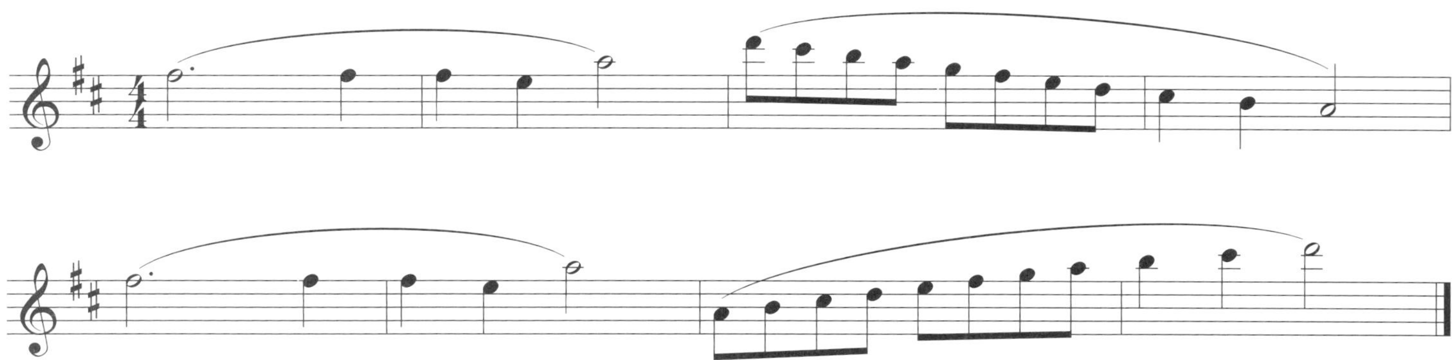

The CD recording (Track 3)

Tune One *is heard played by a bassoon, followed by* **Tune Three** *played by a flute. These represent the two pieces of bread.* **Both tunes** *are then heard played together, representing two pieces of bread laid on top of each other.* **Tune Two** *is heard played alone, by an oboe. It is then placed "between" the two pieces of bread, and represents the sandwich filling. (Listen for the* **three tunes** *played at the same time.)*

The children can hum along with one of the three parts, once they are familiar with the melodies.

- *Listen for the low tune*
- *Listen for the tune in the middle*
- *Listen for the high tune on the top*

Finally, the children could add in their own rhythmic ostinato, which could be just a short recurring pattern, created by themselves, and played lightly on some percussion instruments.

The following melodic ostinato could also be added using pitched percussion

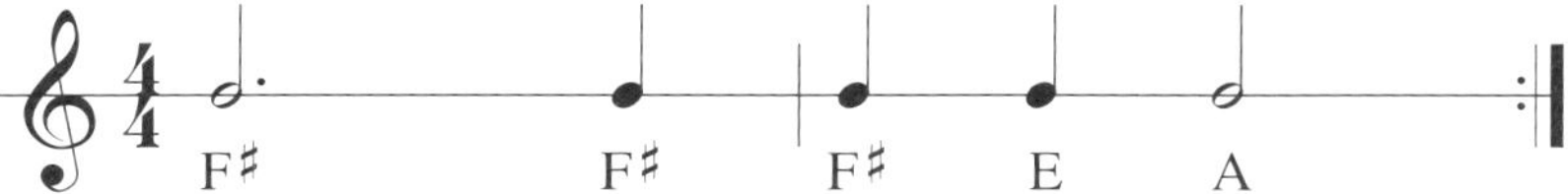

The Musical Sandwich!

SIX FIVE LITTLE DUCKS AND THE TELEPHONE

1. **One little duck sat all alone,**
How he wished his friends would phone.
Then the doorbell began to ring, . . .

Wait for vocal or percussive rings 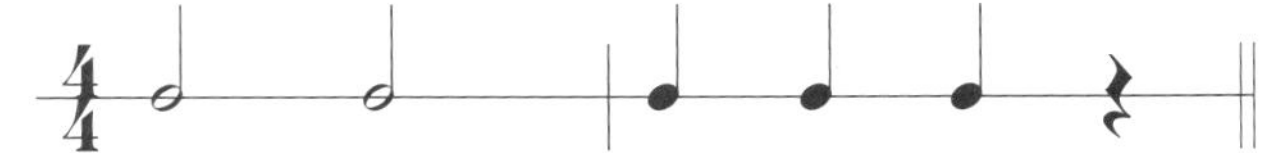

And another little duck came waddling in.
Flap arms with hands on hips, and "quack" to Twinkle Little Star
Quack, quack, quack, quack, quack . . .

2. **Two little ducks sat in a row,**
How they wished the phone would go.
Then the door bell began to ring, . . .

3. **Three little ducks looked really fine**
Sitting neatly in a line.
Then the doorbell began to ring, . . .

4. **Four little ducks sat being good,**
Listening hard, and smiled as they should. (*All smile*)
Then the door bell began to ring, . . .

5. **Five little ducks sat eating their tea,**
Waiting for the phone you see.
Then it rang, and it made them laugh,
All give a hearty laugh and clap hands with delight
For the telephone was ringing out at last.
All make loud and confident telephone ringing noises, or use bells

Telephone noises
Investigation of the ringing tones of most mobile phones will reveal a wealth of different call signs. Practice musical memory, with the children imitating some of them.

Additional fun
Five children can be the ducks and waddle in and sit in a line, on a bench. If they can be obtained, each child could carry a fluffy toy duck or a duck picture they have painted themselves.

SIX FIVE LITTLE DUCKS AND THE TELEPHONE

An action counting song with duck and telephone sounds

Steadily ♩ = 144

C F6 G7 C F6 G7

C Dm G G7 C

1. One lit - tle duck sat all a - lone, how he wished his friends would phone.

F Dm (door bell sound) Dm7

Then the door bell be - gan to ring, *mp* and an -

G F G C 1.2.3.4. C F C

oth - er lit - tle duck came wad - dling in. *f* Quack, quack, quack, quack, quack, quack, quack.

Dm C/G G C To finish

Quack, quack, quack, quack, quack, quack, quack. *f tremolo* **(add phone signals)**

SEVEN PICKING BERRIES

1. **We like picking berries,**
They're juicy, ripe and sweet.
Put them in a basket,
And take them home to eat.

2. **We like eating berries,**
They're juicy, ripe and sweet.
Put them in a pudding bowl,
And then it's time to eat.
Yum, yum! (*Speaking voice*)

Actions:

Verse 1. Pick imaginary berries and carefully put them into a basket, made by crooking one arm.

Verse 2. Rub tummies. Cup hands to represent a pudding bowl. Pick up an imaginary spoon and eat. Yum, yum!

N.B. Please give young children a warning about which berries are suitable to eat!

SEVEN PICKING BERRIES

An action song

*(harvest/food)

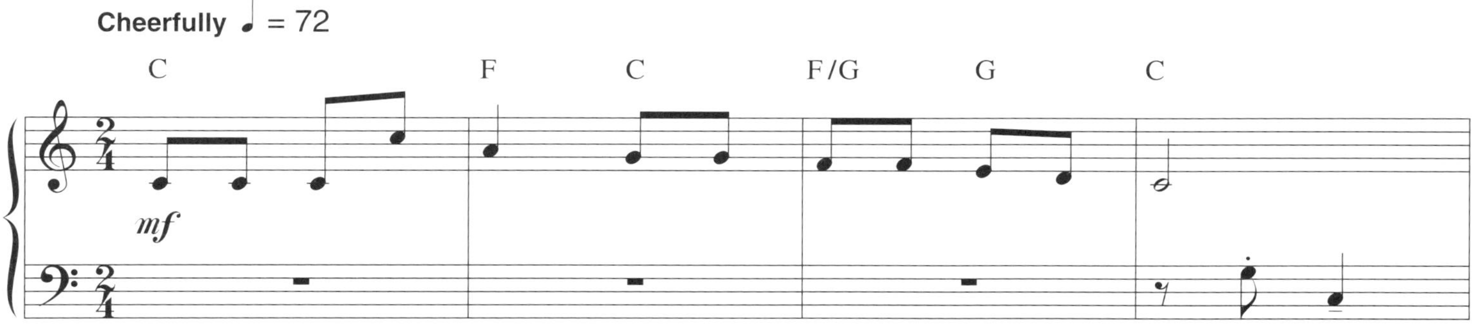

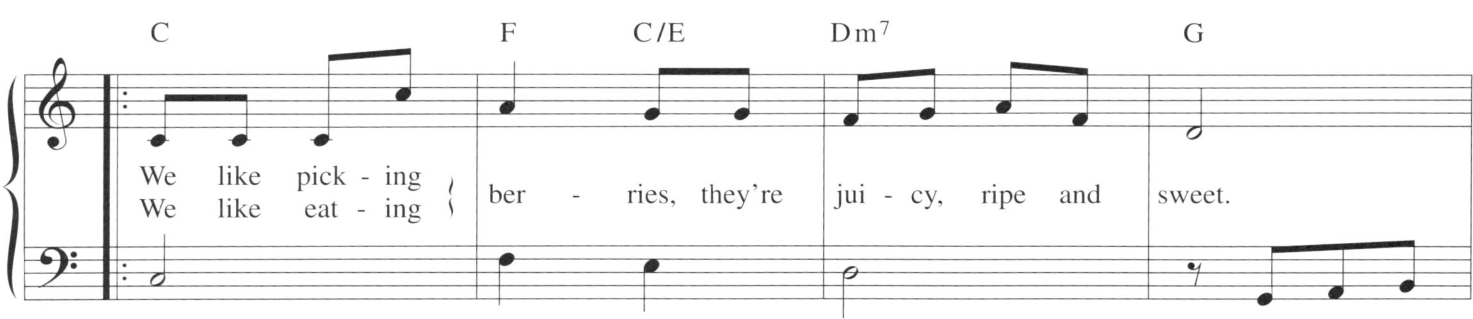

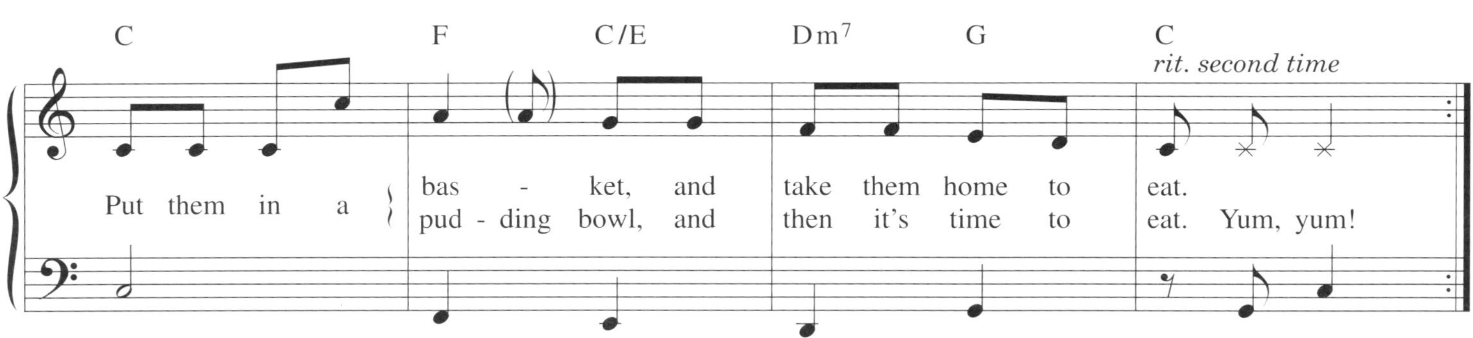

EIGHT IT IS RAINING

First part

It is raining,
It is raining,
It is raining,
It is raining.

Second part

Drip-drop here it comes again.
Drip-drop, plip-plop it is rain.
Drip-drop, splish-splash don't you know
Plants need water to make them grow?
twice

Combine both sections of the song if you would like to sing in two-parts

Actions for the drip-drop words:

Finger falling rain with arms up and slowly dropping down.
Two claps on "splish-splash" and then hands turned outwards in a gesture of questioning.
Arms "grow" up the centre of the body and make a bushy plant.

Chime bar or any pitched percussion notes for playing along with the first part

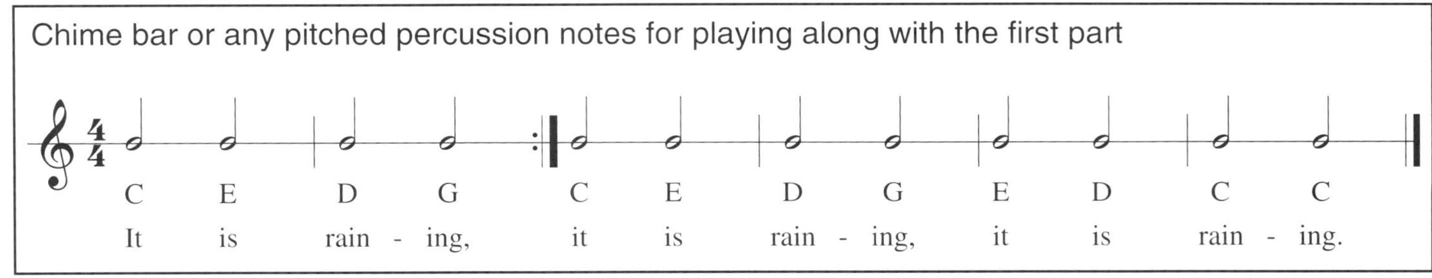

EIGHT IT IS RAINING

An action song with optional chime bars.

Can be sung in two parts.

**(harvest/growth/water)*

Not too fast ♩ = 120

C Db Dm7 G7

mf

C G7 C G7

First Part

It is rain - ing, it is rain - ing,

Second Part

Drip-drop here it comes a - gain.__ Drip-drop, plip-plop it is rain.__

C C/Bb Ddim7 Fm C G

it is rain - ing, it is

Drip - drop, splish-splash, don't you know__ plants need wa - ter to

F C (no chords) C

rain - ing.

make them grow?__

f

NINE LOOKING RIGHT SNAPPY

Actions:

The dance is in two sections – the ***REFRAIN*** *and the* ***VERSES***
All the movements are made in time with the beats, which are at ♩ = 120
The counting is "4" per bar of music, and there are eight bars in each section, and these are marked in the music.
The children stand in a single line, with feet together.

REFRAIN

① *Step forward;*
Right, left, right to three beats.
On the fourth beat, balance on right foot, raise left knee and slap it with right hand

② *Step backwards;*
Left, right, left to three beats.
On the fourth beat balance on left foot, raise right foot behind and slap it with left hand

③ ④ *repeat as above*

⑤ *Step sideways over four counts:*
Right, close left foot to right foot,
Right, close left foot and clap simultaneously

⑥ *Reverse sidestepping:*
Left, close right foot to left,
Left, close right foot to left and clap simultaneously

⑦ ⑧ *Seven little steps on the spot, turning through 360 degrees,*
Clap on final beat

VERSE 1

① ② *Swing right arm in air as if twirling a lasso*

③ *Right heel point to front, (over two beats i.e. slowly)*
Return right foot (over two beats)

④ *Left heel point to front (over two beats)*
Return left foot (over two beats)

⑤ *Step sideways:*
Right, close, right, kick left foot

⑥ *Reverse sidestepping:*
Left, close, left, kick right foot

⑦ ⑧ *Seven little steps on the spot turning through 360 degrees,*
clap on final beat

VERSE 2 ① ② *Bend knees in time with music, and hold hands in front as if holding reins and riding*

③ ④ ⑤ ⑥ ⑦ ⑧ *As for first verse*

Refrain

Looking right snappy,
Bouncy and happy,
Having a good time dancing in line.
Don't mind the weather,
We're stepping together,
All is bright sunshine dancing in line.

1.

Lasso up that roaming steer,
The rodeo will soon be here.
Pay your money for the show,
And wait in line to have a go!

Refrain **Looking right snappy . . .**

2.

Bucking broncos can be fun
Except when you get thrown by one.
Cowboys who can hold on tight
Will entertain the crowd tonight.

Refrain **Looking right snappy . . .**

NINE LOOKING RIGHT SNAPPY

American line dance song

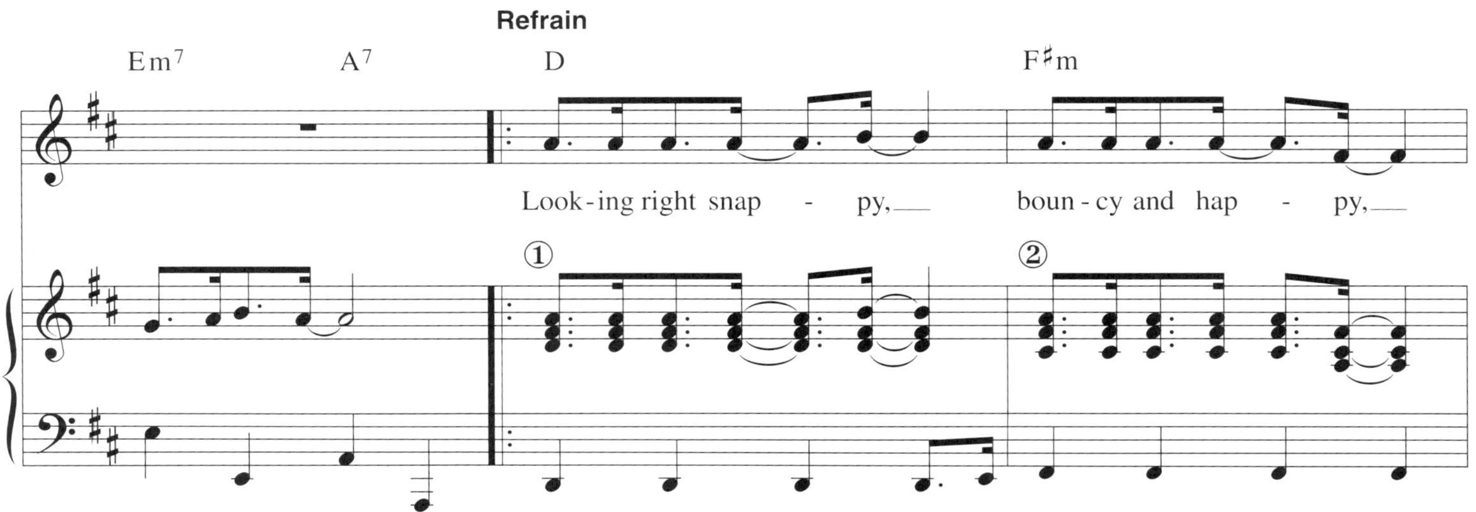

F♯m G Em7 D/A A D
FINE
step-ping to-geth - er, all is bright sun - shine, danc-ing in line.
⑥ ⑦ ⑧
8th
D Em A D
1. Las - so up that roam - ing steer, the ro - de - o will
2. Buck - ing bron - cos can be fun ex - cept when you get
① ② ③
Em A D B
soon be here. Pay your mon - ey for the show, and
thrown by one. Cow - boys who can hold on tight will
④ ⑤ ⑥
Em D/A A F A
wait in line to have a go!
en - ter - tain the crowd to - night.
⑦ ⑧

Other musicals by Alison Hedger

AVAILABLE FROM GOLDEN APPLE

Ballooning Around The World

(Keystage 1+2)
Audience and performers are taken on a balloon journey, visiting Scotland, Russia, Spain, Egypt and Jamaica, exploring food, costumes, music and dance. Includes notes on costume and production, incorporating poetry, recipes and a map of locations.

Teacher's book & CD GA11123

Harvest Time!

(Keystage 1+2)
If you want a celebratory Harvest item for the beginning of term, requiring minimal rehearsal, here is the solution! Each class has their own song in a narrator-led performance. Ideal for involving every child in a meaningful celebration.

Teacher's Book GA11086
Cassette GA11087

Nursery Rhyme Nativity

(Pre-school + Keystage 1)
A delightful retelling of the Nativity story, using the tunes of favourite nursery rhymes, from 'Sing a Song of Sixpence' to 'Hot Cross Buns'. Easy to learn and stage - and an ideal end-of-term item for very young children.

Teacher's book & CD GA11108

AVAILABLE FROM CHESTER

Ocarina Choo-Choo!

An exiting new series to let even your youngest pupils discover the fun of playing music together, whilst laying a firm base of musical understanding. Includes teaching on traditional notation, terms and signs, scales, arpeggios, part-playing and chord work, with the ocarina being ideal for teaching young people music in a progression to recorder playing.

Ocarina Choo-Choo 1 Getting Started CH61740
Ocarina Choo-Choo 2 Learning More CH61741
Ocarina Choo-Choo 1 Getting Started with CD CH61679
Ocarina Choo-Choo 2 Learning More with CD CH61680

Music Sales Limited Newmarket Road, Bury St. Edmunds, Suffolk, IP33 3YB